T0417723

# HEALTHY BODY

by Kirsty Holmes

BEARPORT
PUBLISHING

Minneapolis, Minnesota

## Credits

Images are courtesy of Shutterstock.com. With thanks to GettyImages, ThinkstockPhoto, and iStockphoto. Recurring images – gravity_point, adecvatman, Gaidamashchuk, Zakharchenko Anna, Elena Pimukova. Cover – Inspiring, inspiring.team, Akira1592, Banana Walking, Inkley Studio, myboys.me, Sylfida. 2–3 – Take Photo. 4–5 – Chay_Tee, Inkley Studio, PeopleImages.com – Yuri A, Lapina, Prostock-studio, Valentina Sabelskaia. 6–7 – Antonov Maxim, BearFotos, DragonTiger8, Khrystyna KL, Seita. 8–9 – Bohdan Malitskiy, Galushko Sergey, inspiring.team, Krakenimages.com, Pogorelova Olga, Rawpixel.com, Roman Samborskyi. 10–11 – Akira1592, Bibadash, Billion Photos, FAMILY STOCK, Mastaco, NDAB Creativity, Sylfida. 12–13 – aappp, Bahau, graphixmania, Kameel4u, MaryDesy, Monkey Business Images, Tatjana Baibakova. 14–15 – graphixmania, Anton Nalivayko, Choksawatdikorn, Fagreia, Nomad_Soul, Rob Marmion. 16–17 – Achiichiii, boxstock, Magic mine, MattL_Images, New Africa, wowomnom. 18–19 – Asier Romero, Explode, Martial Red, New Africa, Pikovit, stockcreations. 20–21 – Africa Studio, Amahce, APIRAKKA, lukpedclub, MDGRPHCS, paffy, ValloneArt. 22–23 – inspiring.team, Macrovector, Prostock-studio, Tatjana Baibakova. 24–25 – Colorfuel Studio, Inkley Studio, Krakenimages.com, Pixel-Shot, Roman3dArt, Torgado. 26–27 – Dedraw Studio, Goncharov_Artem, Kakigori Studio, New Africa, Nolte Lourens, Peakstock, Xavier Lorenzo. 28–29 – MaryDesy, Monkey Business Images, Rudenko Alla, Tartila, Teran Studios. 30 – Net Vector, Rob Marmion, Roman Samborskyi.

Library of Congress Cataloging-in-Publication Data is available at www.loc.gov or upon request from the publisher.

ISBN: 979-8-88916-461-6 (hardcover)
ISBN: 979-8-88916-466-1 (paperback)
ISBN: 979-8-88916-470-8 (ebook)

© 2024 BookLife Publishing
This edition is published by arrangement with BookLife Publishing.

For more information, write to Bearport Publishing, 5357 Penn Avenue South, Minneapolis, MN 55419.

# CONTENTS

# Healthy Living

## WHAT IS A LIFESTYLE?

Your lifestyle is the way that you live your life. It includes everything from what you eat to your favorite activities. There are many kinds of lifestyles because people are all different.

## A HEALTHY BODY

Maintaining a healthy body is part of having a healthy lifestyle. There are many ways to help your body be its best. They include eating well, getting exercise, and resting enough.

KEEPING YOUR BODY CLEAN IS ALSO IMPORTANT.

## A **HEALTHY** MIND

A healthy lifestyle means taking care of your mind, too. Spending time with your friends and family keeps your relationships strong. Taking time to relax and doing things you enjoy are great ways to keep your mind happy.

**WHAT ARE SOME OF YOUR FAVORITE ACTIVITIES OR HOBBIES?**

**YOU CAN'T TELL IF SOMEONE IS HEALTHY BY LOOKING AT THEM. BEING HEALTHY IS DIFFERENT FOR EVERYONE.**

## **MAKING** HEALTHY **CHOICES**

Your lifestyle is made up of many choices. What kinds of food do you eat? How do you stay active? Do you spend time with your friends? You don't need to make the perfect choice every time to have a healthy lifestyle. However, it's important to understand how different choices might make you feel.

5

# THE BODY

## AMANZING BODIES

Your body does many amazing things. You use it to get around, eat, play, and think. You can even use your body to bake a cake or play sports. But your body also works hard to keep you alive and healthy. Each and every part of your body is important.

## ORGANS

Organs are body parts with jobs. Organs on the inside of your body, including your heart and lungs, are called **internal** organs. There are also organs on the outside of your body, such as your eyes and skin.

THE LARGEST ORGAN YOU HAVE IS YOUR SKIN. IT HELPS KEEP **GERMS** OUT.

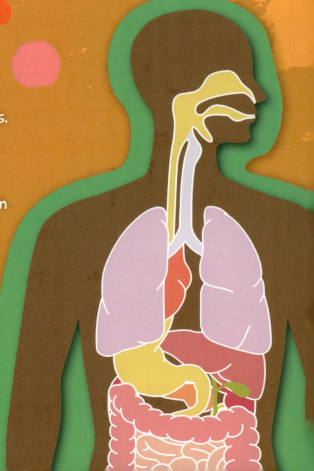

# BODY SYSTEMS

Organs each have a job to do on their own, but sometimes they also work together in body systems. You have systems for moving around, eating, sensing the world, breathing, and more.

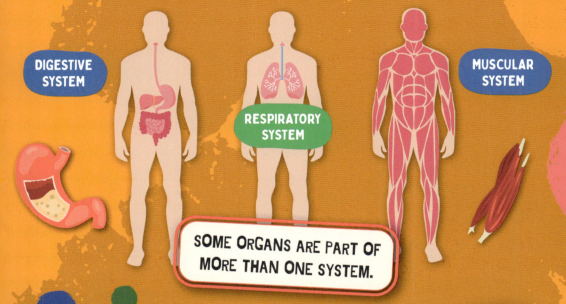

**DIGESTIVE SYSTEM**

**RESPIRATORY SYSTEM**

**MUSCULAR SYSTEM**

SOME ORGANS ARE PART OF MORE THAN ONE SYSTEM.

## LOOKING AFTER YOUR BODY

Sometimes, bodies get sick, injured, or tired. When you aren't feeling well, your body may not be working at its best. It's important to listen to your body to know when it needs to rest and recover.

# THE SENSES

Some of your organs give you information about what's going on around you. The different ways your body gets this information are called the senses.

## SIGHT

Your eyes let you see things. They sense light, shapes, colors, and more.

SOME PEOPLE NEED TO WEAR GLASSES TO HELP THEM SEE BETTER.

## HEARING

Tiny bones and hairs inside your ears allow you to hear sounds.

PEOPLE WHO ARE DEAF OR HARD OF HEARING MAY USE HEARING AIDS TO HELP THEM USE THIS SENSE.

## SMELL

Your nose allows you to smell different things. It senses **particles** in the air.

## TASTE

Small bumps on your tongue called taste buds sense flavors. They help you taste sweet, sour, salty, bitter, and **umami** foods.

YOUR SENSES OF SMELL AND TASTE WORK TOGETHER. BEING ABLE TO SMELL YOUR FOOD ALLOWS YOU TO TASTE IT MORE FULLY.

## TOUCH

Your skin has special cells that sense the textures and temperatures of things you touch. This information is then sent to your brain.

9

# THE IMMUNE SYSTEM

## GERMS

There are many different kinds of germs. Most are harmless, but some can cause trouble if they get inside your body. These germs are called **pathogens**.

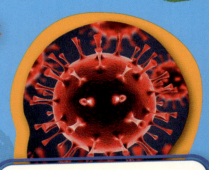

> PATHOGENS ARE VERY TINY AND CAN BE SEEN ONLY WITH A MICROSCOPE.

## GETTING SICK

There are many ways pathogens might get into your body. They could be in the air you breathe, on the surfaces you touch, or even in the food you eat. When you get sick from a pathogen, you have an infection. Sick people can spread the pathogen to other people.

> INFECTIONS CAN MAKE YOU FEEL UNWELL. **SYMPTOMS** CAN INCLUDE A RUNNY NOSE OR A FEVER.

# YOUR IMMUNE SYSTEM

Luckily, you have an immune system. Its main job is to protect you from pathogens. Your immune system is made up of organs and cells that work together to find and destroy any pathogens that get into your body.

WHEN YOU ARE SICK, A DOCTOR MAY BE ABLE TO HELP YOU FEEL BETTER WITH MEDICINE.

# PREVENTING AND TREATING ILLNESSES

You can protect yourself and others against pathogens with a few easy steps:

- Wash your hands well and often.
- Wear a mask if you are around sick people.
- Stay away from others if you are sick.
- Get vaccines, such as the flu shot, to help teach your immune system to attack pathogens.

# BONES

## THE SKELETAL SYSTEM

Your skeleton is all the bones in your body. The skeletal system holds your body up, protects internal organs, and gives your body its shape.

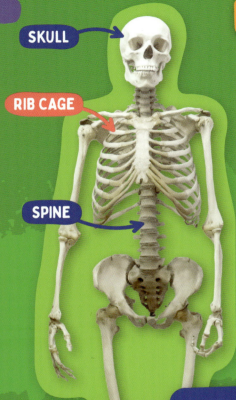

SKULL

RIB CAGE

SPINE

TIBIA AND FIBULA

BABIES ARE BORN WITH ABOUT 270 BONES. AS THEY GROW, SOME BONES **FUSE** TOGETHER. ADULTS END UP WITH ABOUT 206 BONES.

## BONES

You have lots of different bones, from the skull in your head to the tibia and fibula in your legs. Many small bones make up the spine that runs down the middle of your back, and the bones of your rib cage wrap around in your chest.

THE PLACES WHERE TWO BONES MEET ARE CALLED JOINTS. JOINTS, SUCH AS YOUR ELBOWS, KNEES, AND WRISTS, HELP YOU BEND AND MOVE.

## BREAKING BONES

If a bone breaks, it's called a fracture. A doctor may wrap the part of your body with the fracture in a hard covering called a cast. This keeps it still. They may also give you crutches to help you walk. A broken bone needs rest so it can heal itself.

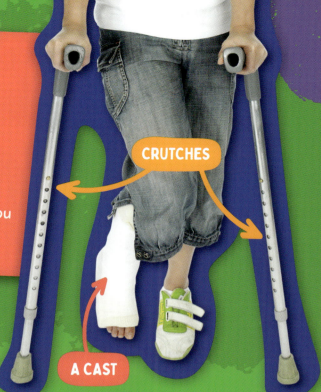

CRUTCHES

A CAST

## BUILDING BETTER BONES

There are simple things you can do to make your bones stronger and less likely to break. Smart lifestyle choices can keep your bones healthy.

• Eat calcium-rich foods, such as dairy, green veggies, or nuts.
• Get vitamin D by spending time in sunshine. Also look for it in **fortified** foods.
• Exercise regularly.

EGGS, NUTS, CHEESES, AND MANY FRUITS AND VEGETABLES ARE GOOD FOR YOUR BONES!

# MUSCLES

## WHAT ARE MUSCLES?

Without muscles, you wouldn't get far. Muscles hold your skeleton together and make it move. They are attached to your bones with tendons.

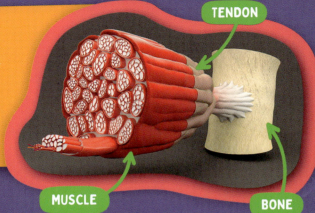

TENDON

MUSCLE

BONE

YOU HAVE ABOUT 600 DIFFERENT MUSCLES IN YOUR BODY.

## MAKING YOU MOVE

Your muscles move body parts by bunching up and pulling bones. Many muscles work in pairs, one that pulls a bone in one direction and another that pulls it back. A muscle that pulls a bone to bend a **limb** is called a flexor. A muscle that pulls to straighten a limb is called an extensor.

# MUSCLE INJURIES

Your muscles work really hard. The muscular system is responsible for all kinds of movement, from beating your heart and smiling to running and jumping. But muscles can get sore when you use them a lot. You can also overstretch a muscle and tear it.

YOGA IS A GREAT ACTIVITY TO GENTLY STRETCH YOUR MUSCLES.

## YOUR HEALTHY MUSCLES

There are many things you can do to keep your muscles strong.

- Eat protein-rich foods, such as meat, fish, beans, and eggs.
- Stretch and move regularly.
- Rest your muscles when they need time to heal.

# THE BRAIN

Your brain is a wrinkly organ inside your head. It's in charge of . . . well, everything! It helps you think and feel. Your brain also tells your other body systems what to do. It tells your muscles to move and helps you process the information you get from your senses.

**YOUR BRAIN IS WHERE YOUR THOUGHTS COME FROM.**

## THE LEARNING CENTER

All you do relies on connections between different parts of your brain. Learning a new skill can feel difficult at first. This is because new connections are being formed in your brain. As you practice, those connections grow stronger. Soon, the skill becomes easy!

**BRAIN CELLS CALLED NEURONS MAKE A TINY BIT OF ELECTRICITY WHEN YOU THINK. YOUR WHOLE BRAIN CAN MAKE ENOUGH ELECTRICITY TO POWER A LIGHT BULB!**

# THE CENTRAL NERVOUS SYSTEM

The central nervous system controls your whole body. Your brain teams up with the **nerves** running down the spinal cord in your back. This system carries information and messages back and forth between your brain and the rest of your body.

YOUR BRAIN NEEDS OXYGEN, WATER, EXERCISE, AND SLEEP TO STAY HEALTHY.

## BEST FOR THE BRAIN

Your brain needs a lot of energy to do so much work. It gets most of this energy from a type of sugar called glucose. Pasta, oatmeal, and whole grain breads are all good sources of glucose.

# LUNGS

## BREATHE EASY

You have a pair of lungs in your chest. They are similar to soft, baggy balloons. When you breathe in, your lungs fill with air and your body takes in oxygen. Your body needs this gas to stay alive.

THE LUNGS ARE THE MAIN ORGAN OF YOUR RESPIRATORY SYSTEM.

## THE DIAPHRAGM

Your lungs have a little bit of help to work. The diaphragm is a large muscle under your lungs. When you inhale, it moves away from your lungs to let them fill with air. To exhale, the diaphragm relaxes and pushes the air back out.

## HARD TO BREATHE

Some people can have problems with their lungs that can lead to coughing, chest pain, and difficulty breathing. Asthma is one common problem that causes the chest to feel tight and makes breathing difficult.

INHALER

IF YOU HAVE ASTHMA, A DOCTOR MIGHT GIVE YOU AN INHALER THAT HAS MEDICINE FOR YOUR LUNGS.

## LOOK AFTER THE LUNGS

When you breathe, you take in whatever is in the air around you. This might include pathogens or things that can irritate your lungs, such as pollen or smoke. Taking care of your lungs means being aware of what goes into them.

WEARING A MASK CAN HELP STOP YOU FROM INHALING PATHOGENS.

19

# THE HEART

## PUMP IT UP

Your heart is an organ in the left side of your chest that's made of very strong muscles. Its job is to pump blood all around your body. As it does, it sends the oxygen you need throughout your body.

YOUR BRAIN TELLS YOUR HEART TO BEAT WITHOUT YOU EVEN HAVING TO THINK ABOUT IT.

## TO THE BEAT

Each time your heart pumps, you feel it as a beat. These heartbeats make up your pulse. You can check your pulse by pressing your fingertips along the inside of your wrist. You should be able to feel a *thump-thump* against your fingers.

WHEN YOU EXERCISE, YOUR HEART BEATS FASTER TO GET YOUR BODY MORE OXYGEN.

# THE CIRCULATORY SYSTEM

The heart pumps blood around the body in a network of little tubes called blood vessels. Together with the heart and lungs, they form the circulatory system. There are three kinds of blood vessels.

## ARTERIES

The heart pumps oxygen-rich blood through arteries toward your muscles and organs.

## VEINS

Veins carry blood from the body to the heart where it can be sent to the lungs to pick up oxygen.

## CAPILLARIES

Capillaries are small tubes that branch off from the arteries to deliver oxygen-rich blood to your muscles and organs.

## LOVE YOUR HEART

What you eat can help your heart! Eating fruits, vegetables, **lean** meats, oily fish, and whole grains can keep your heart at its best.

# THE DIGESTIVE SYSTEM

## WHAT'S IN MY FOOD?

Your body needs **nutrients** to live, grow, and make energy. Nutrients, including vitamins, proteins, and carbohydrates are in the food you eat. In order to get them, however, your body needs to do a little work first.

**MOUTH**

**ESOPHAGUS**

**STOMACH**

**INTESTINES**

## THE DIGESTIVE SYSTEM

The different organs of the digestive system work together to break down food. First, the mouth chews the food to break it into smaller bits. Once swallowed, food goes down your esophagus and into your stomach, where **acids** turn it into a watery mush that then moves into the intestines.

FOOD CAN TRAVEL AS FAR AS 30 FEET (9 M) INSIDE YOUR DIGESTIVE SYSTEM.

## TUMMY TROUBLES

Old food or pathogens can cause stomach pains, cramps, nausea, diarrhea, or vomiting. Some people can also have food intolerances that can make them feel unwell.

STOMACH PAIN AND GAS CAN SOMETIMES BE CAUSED BY INDIGESTION. THIS HAPPENS IF FOOD ISN'T BROKEN DOWN PROPERLY.

## SUPER STOMACH CARE

Fiber is something your digestive system needs to work well. It is found in some plant-based foods, including whole grains, fruits, and vegetables. Fiber helps move food through the intestines and out of your body.

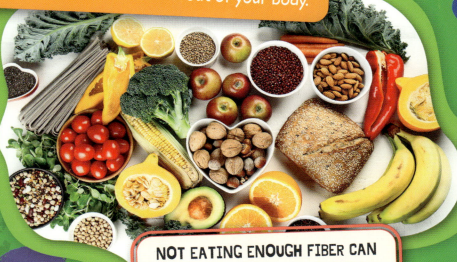

NOT EATING ENOUGH FIBER CAN MAKE IT DIFFICULT TO POOP! THIS CAN BE VERY UNCOMFORTABLE.

# THE MOUTH

## SUCH A MOUTHFUL!

### INCISORS
Incisors are the sharp, thin teeth at the front of your mouth. They help you bite into and cut up your food.

### CANINES
You have pointy canines on either side of your incisors. They are used to tear into tough food.

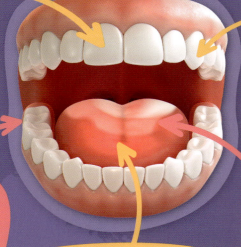

### MOLARS
These are the large, flat teeth at the back of your mouth. They help you grind food into a paste.

### TONGUE
Your tongue tastes food, moves it around, mashes it, and pushes it to the back of your mouth to be swallowed. It is also used for speaking.

### SALIVA
Saliva mixes with your food and helps to break it down.

HUMANS ARE BORN WITH BABY TEETH THAT FALL **OUT** AND ARE REPLACED BY ADULT TEETH.

## MOUTH **MATTERS**

Problems with your teeth can lead to bad breath, sore gums, and tooth **decay**. Teeth that are decaying can be very painful. They can also get cavities, which makes them sensitive to cold temperatures and sugary foods. Taking care of your teeth can help you avoid these problems.

A DENTIST CAN HELP IF YOU ARE HAVING PROBLEMS WITH YOUR TEETH.

## **DENTAL** HYGIENE

Once you have your adult teeth, you don't get any more. That's why it's so important to take care of them! Brush your teeth and tongue twice a day. Floss at least once a day, making sure to get in around each tooth.

REGULAR VISITS TO A DENTIST WILL HELP KEEP YOUR MOUTH IN GREAT SHAPE.

25

# DIFFERENT BODIES

## MY BODY, YOUR BODY, EVERY BODY

Most bodies have the same organs and body systems, but we're all a little different. We all have different hair, skin colors, and heights. Every body is unique!

## BETTER TOGETHER

Each body is built differently, with its own strengths and challenges. Something that is easy for you, might be difficult for someone else. Working together to overcome challenges makes us stronger as a group.

**WHAT ARE SOME OF YOUR STRENGTHS AND CHALLENGES?**

## DISABILITIES

A disability is something about the body that makes it hard to do certain things, such as moving or sensing the world. There are lots of different kinds of disabilities.

## ACCOMMODATIONS

There are many gadgets that make the world more accessible to people of all abilities. Some people may use wheelchairs or walking sticks to help them move around. Other people use hearing aids or glasses to help them hear and see.

**HEARING AID**

SOMETHING THAT HELPS YOU MOVE AROUND, SUCH AS CRUTCHES, IS CALLED A MOBILITY AID.

NOT ALL DISABILITIES CAN BE SEEN. SOME ARE INSIDE THE BODY OR THE BRAIN.

# LOOKING AFTER your BODY

You only get one body, so it's important to take care of it.

## MOVE IT

Your body needs plenty of exercise to stay healthy. Playing a sport, dancing, and playing with your friends are great ways to get your body moving.

## FEED IT!

A balanced diet will give your body energy. It will help you grow and keep you healthy. Try to eat lots of fruits and veggies and have a variety of foods on your plate. And don't forget to drink plenty of water!

**YOU NEED 6 TO 8 GLASSES OF WATER EVERY DAY!**

## KEEP IT CLEAN!

Keeping your body clean can help you to stay healthy. Brush your teeth, wash your skin and hair, and keep your fingernails short so they don't trap in dirt.

CLEANING YOUR BODY REGULARLY HELPS GET RID OF GERMS AND DIRT.

## GIVE IT SOME LOVE

Every body is a good body, and yours is unique to you. That means you may need different things than your friends do to stay healthy and strong. Taking care of your body is an important part of your healthy lifestyle!

29

# MY BODY, MY RULES

A healthy lifestyle is all about making choices. Taking care of your organs and body systems is an important part of living well!

**NO**

IF ANYONE NEEDS TO TOUCH YOU TO HELP YOU, THEY SHOULD ASK YOU FIRST AND TELL YOU WHAT THEY ARE GOING TO DO.

REGULAR VISITS TO THE DOCTOR AND DENTIST CAN HELP YOU LOOK AFTER YOUR BODY!

## IF I SAY SO

The best thing about your body is that it's all yours. You are in charge of it, and you get to say what happens to it. Other people should ask permission before touching you and must respect your choice if you say no.

# GLOSSARY

**acids**  chemicals that can break things down

**decay**  to rot

**fortified**  supplemented with vitamins and minerals to make food more nutritious

**fuse**  to join together

**germs**  tiny living things, including bacteria and viruses, that can make you sick

**internal**  inside your body

**lean**  having little or no fat

**limb**  an arm or leg

**nerves**  parts of the body that send messages from the brain to other parts of the body

**nutrients**  vitamins, minerals, and other substances needed by living things to stay healthy and grow

**oxygen**  a gas in the air that people need to live

**particles**  tiny pieces of something

**pathogens**  germs that cause illnesses

**symptoms**  signs of an illness, such as a cough, fever, or rash

**umami**  a rich flavor found in many foods

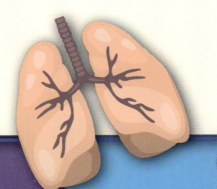

# INDEX

# READ MORE

**Choi, Betty.** *Human Body Learning Lab: Take an inside Tour of How Your Anatomy Works.* North Adams, MA: Storey Publishing, 2022.

**Finan, Catherine C.** *The Human Body (X-treme Facts: Science).* Minneapolis: Bearport Publishing Company, 2021.

# LEARN MORE ONLINE

1. Go to **www.factsurfer.com** or scan the QR code below.

2. Enter "**Healthy Body**" into the search box.

3. Click on the cover of this book to see a list of websites.